Doctor Tools

by Laura Hamilton Waxman

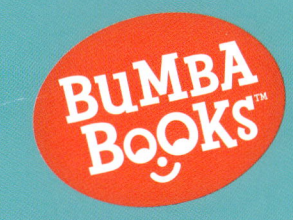

BUMBA BOOKS

LERNER PUBLICATIONS ◆ MINNEAPOLIS

Note to Educators

Throughout this book, you'll find critical-thinking questions. These can be used to engage young readers in thinking critically about the topic and in using the text and photos to do so.

Copyright © 2020 by Lerner Publishing Group, Inc.

All rights reserved. International copyright secured. No part of this book may be reproduced, stored in a retrieval system, or transmitted in any form or by any means—electronic, mechanical, photocopying, recording, or otherwise—without the prior written permission of Lerner Publishing Group, Inc., except for the inclusion of brief quotations in an acknowledged review.

Lerner Publications Company
A division of Lerner Publishing Group, Inc.
241 First Avenue North
Minneapolis, MN 55401 USA

For reading levels and more information, look up this title at www.lernerbooks.com.

Main body text set in Helvetica Textbook Com Roman 23/49.
Typeface provided by Linotype AG.

Library of Congress Cataloging-in-Publication Data

Names: Waxman, Laura Hamilton, author.
Title: Doctor tools / by Laura Hamilton Waxman.
Description: Minneapolis : Lerner Publications, [2020] | Series: Bumba books. Community helpers tools of the trade | Includes bibliographical references and index. | Audience: Age 4–7. | Audience: K to Grade 3.
Identifiers: LCCN 2018047582 (print) | LCCN 2018051182 (ebook) | ISBN 9781541557345 (eb pdf) | ISBN 9781541557338 (lb : alk. paper) | ISBN 9781541573505 (pb : alk. paper)
Subjects: LCSH: Physicians—Juvenile literature. | Medical instruments and apparatus—Juvenile literature. | Children—Medical examinations—Juvenile literature.
Classification: LCC R856.2 (ebook) | LCC R856.2 .W39 2020 (print) | DDC 610.28/4—dc23

LC record available at https://lccn.loc.gov/2018047582

Manufactured in the United States of America
1-46148-45897-1/11/2019

Table of Contents

Let's Visit a Doctor! 4

Doctor Tools 22

Picture Glossary 23

Read More 24

Index 24

Let's Visit a Doctor!

Doctors help sick people.

They use tools to keep us healthy.

5

6

Many doctors wear white coats.

They may also wear gloves.

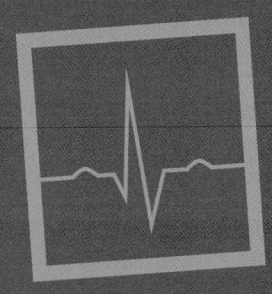

A doctor uses an exam table.

Patients sit on this table.

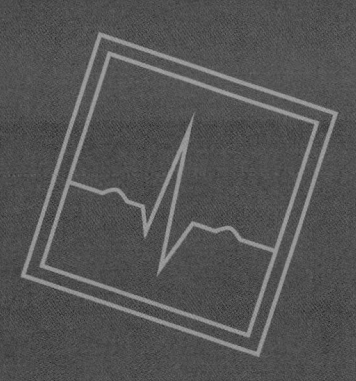

9

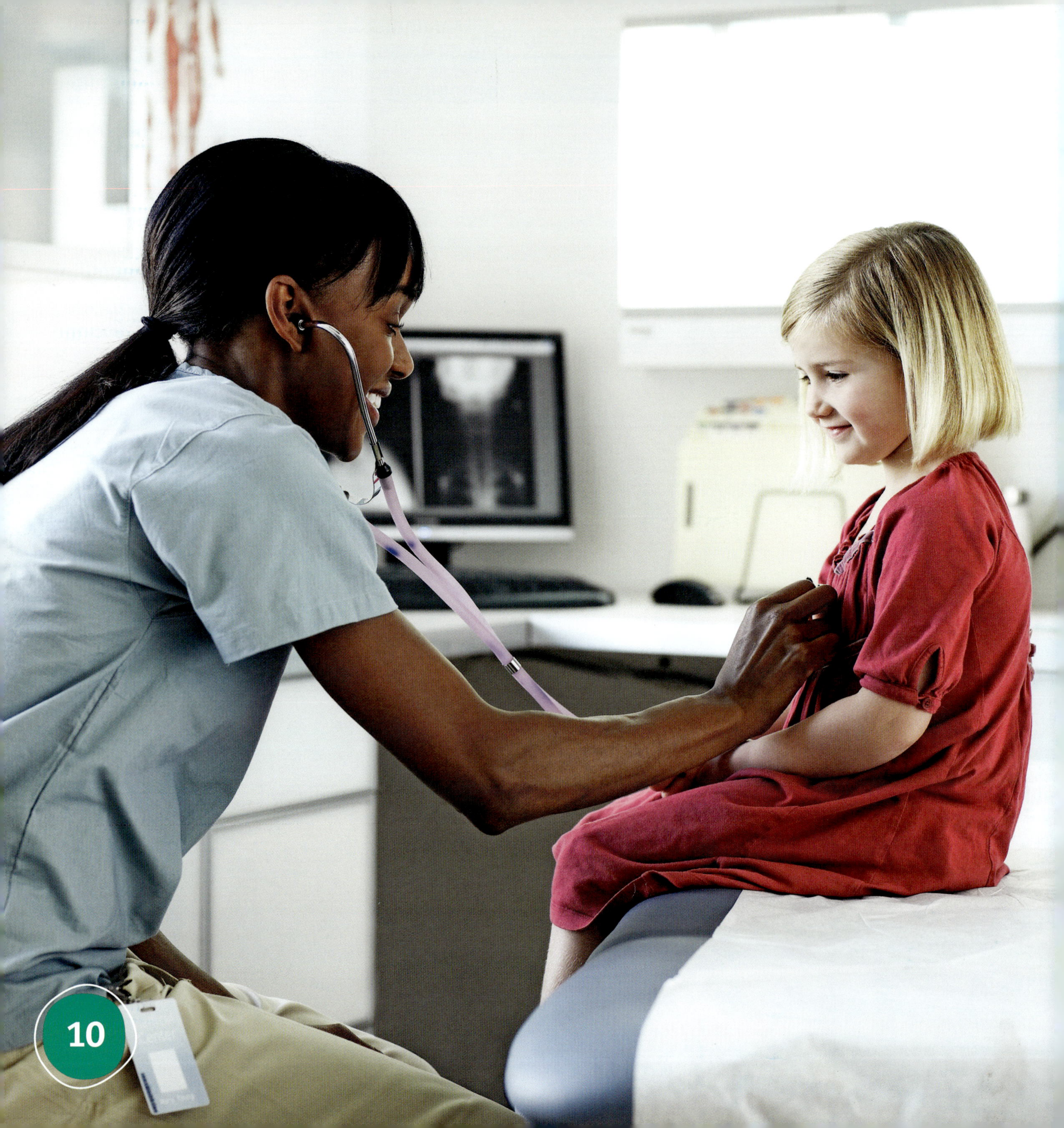

Doctors use a stethoscope.

They use it to listen to your heart.

They also listen to your lungs.

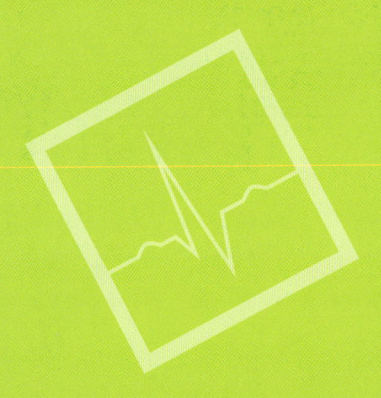

Sometimes doctors need to see inside a patient's ear.

A special tool lets them look inside.

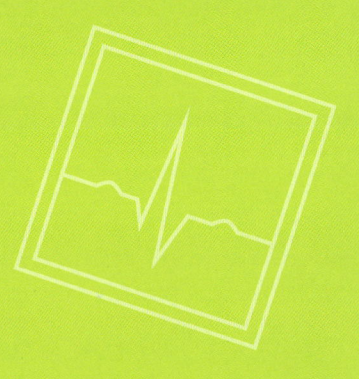

13

14

Doctors use a wooden tool to push down your tongue.

It helps a doctor see your throat.

Why might doctors look at your throat?

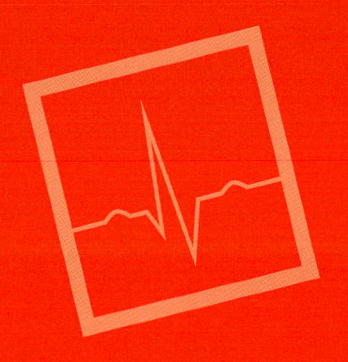

X-rays show the inside of a patient's body.

They show if a bone is broken.

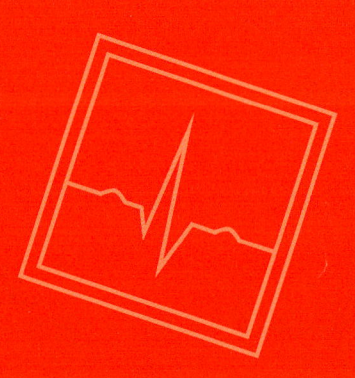

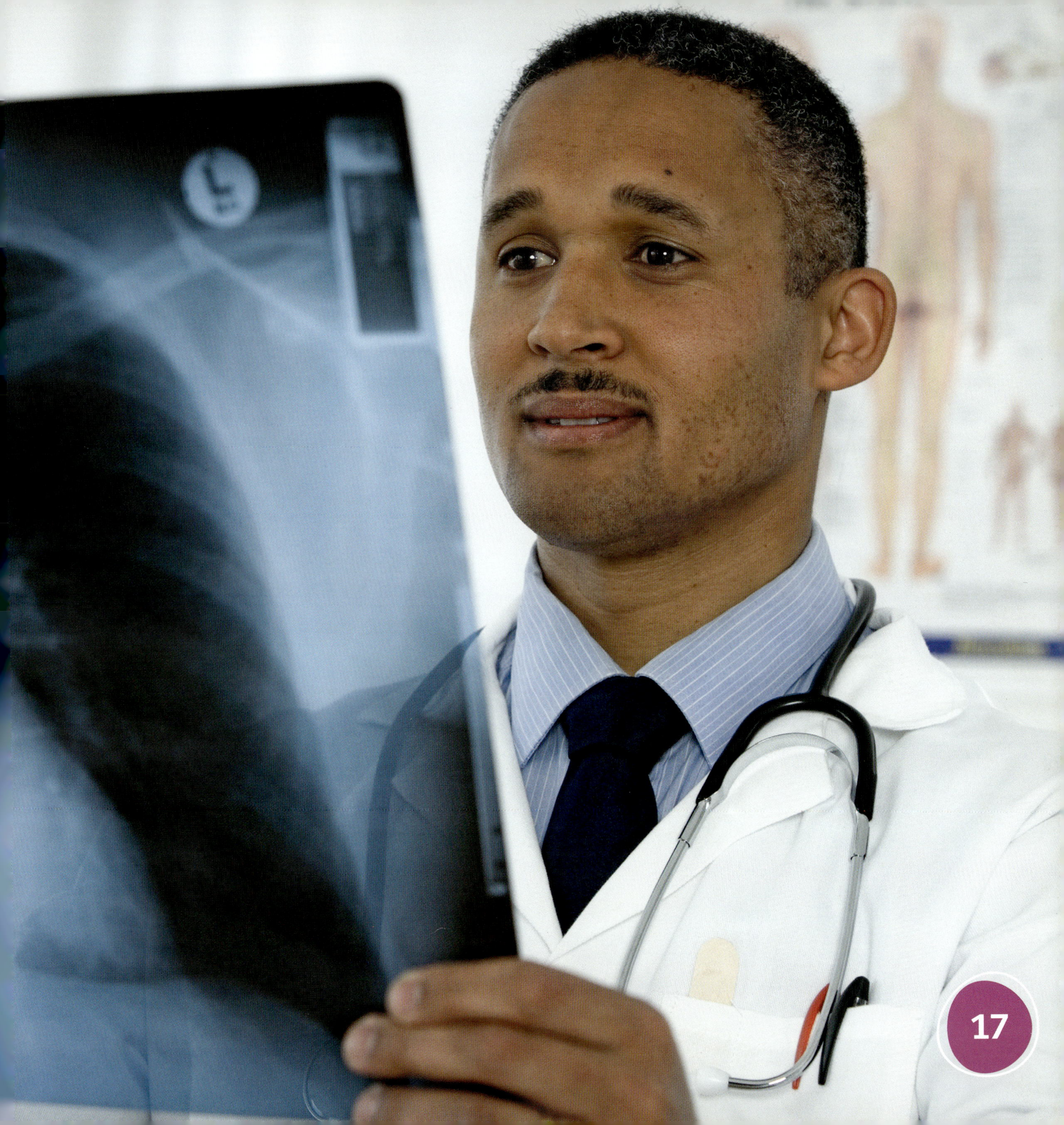

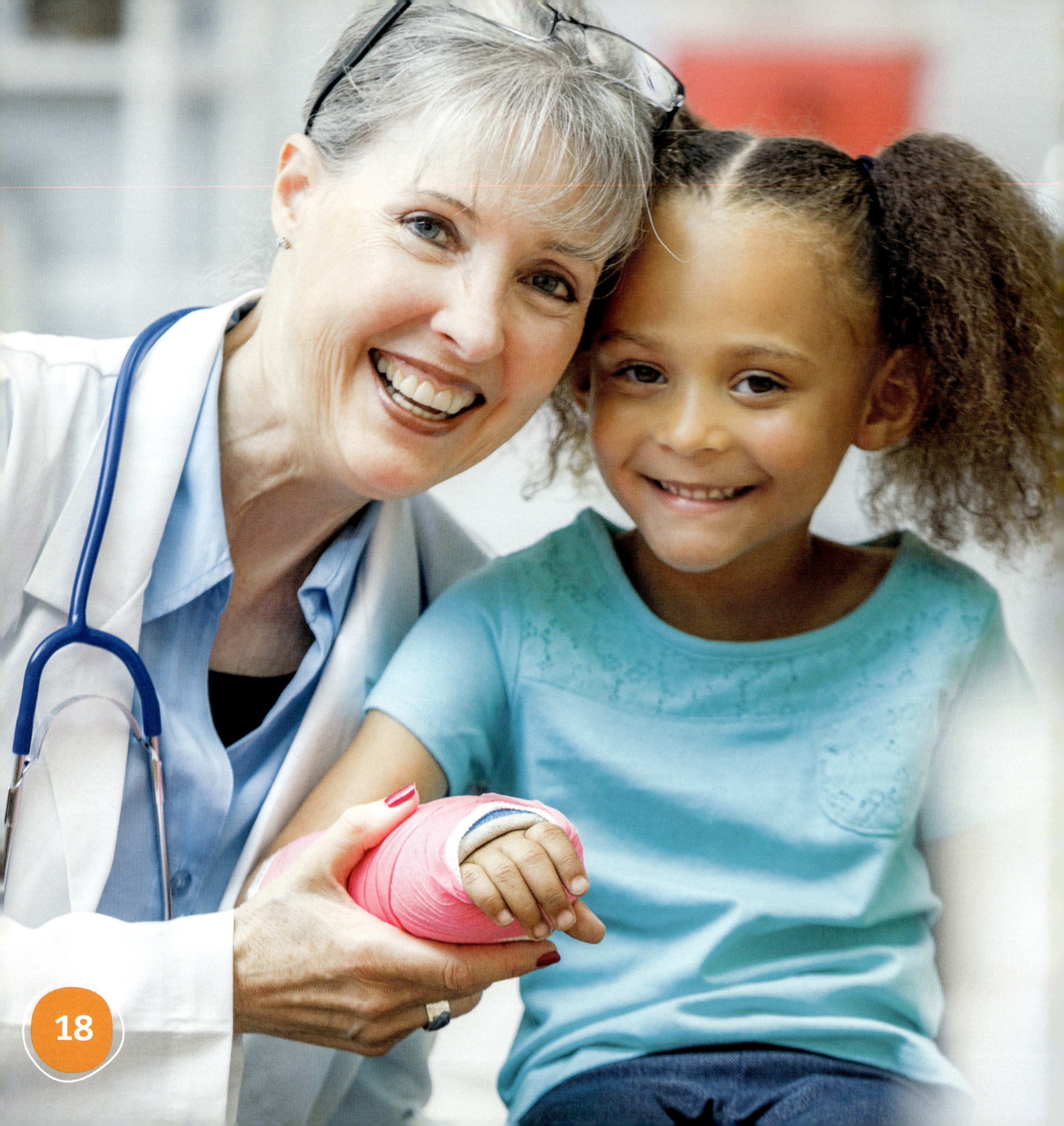

Doctors use casts to heal broken bones.

They use bandages to help heal cuts.

How might casts and bandages help people heal?

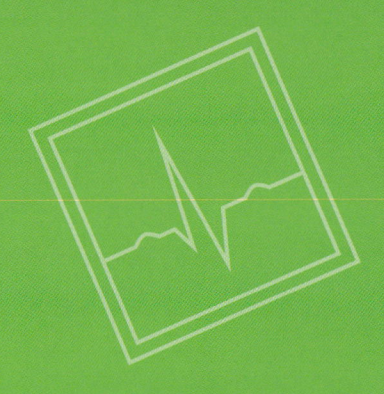

Sometimes doctors give you medicine to make you feel better. Doctors use many tools to keep you healthy!

21

Doctor Tools

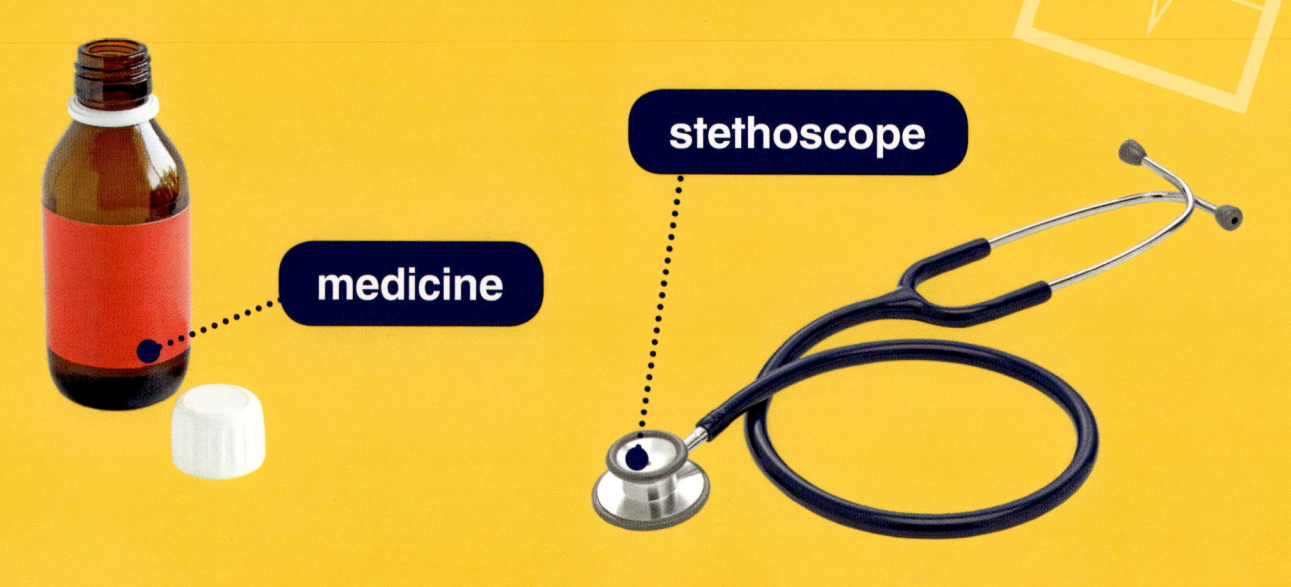

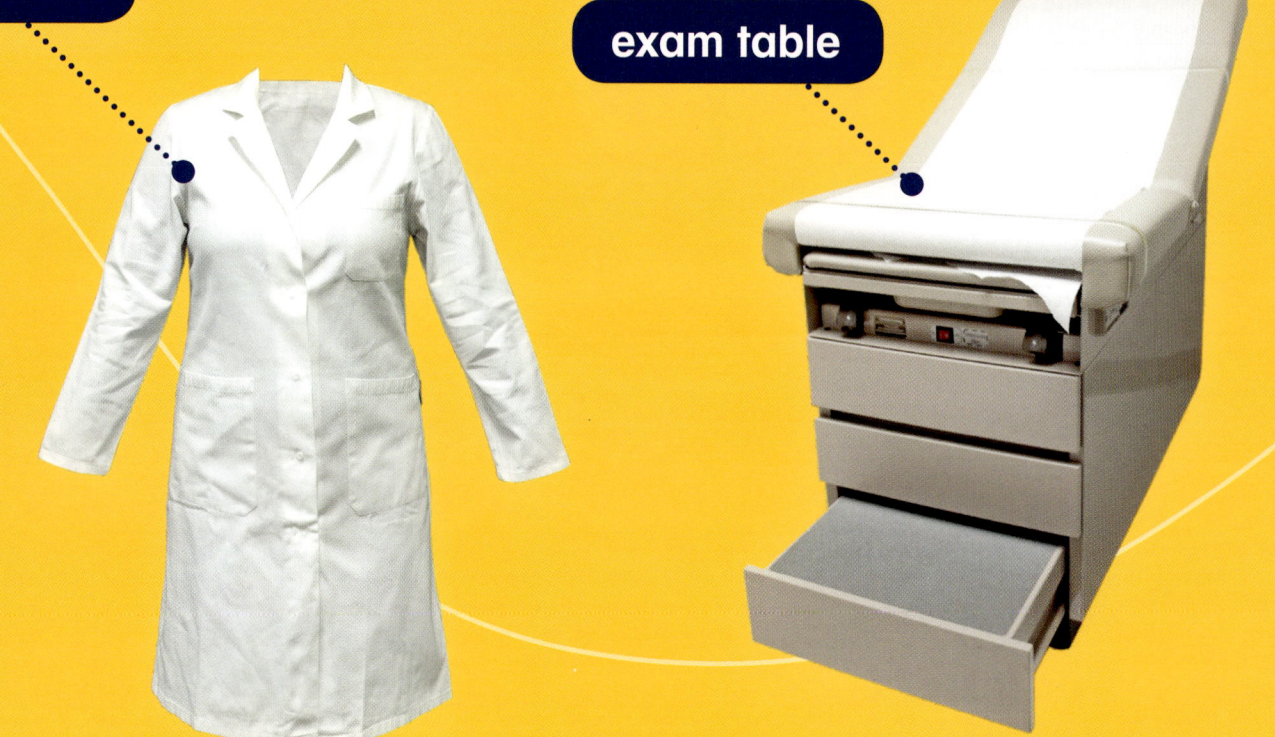

- medicine
- stethoscope
- white coat
- exam table

Picture Glossary

casts — hard bandages that are put around broken bones

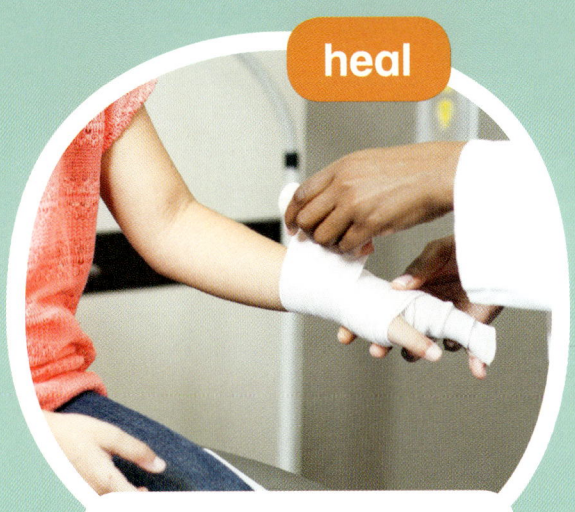

heal — to get better after being sick or hurt

patients — people who visit doctors

stethoscope — a tool used to listen to someone's heart and lungs

Read More

Clark, Rosalyn. *Why We Go to the Doctor.* Minneapolis: Lerner Publications, 2018.

Heos, Bridget. *Doctors in My Community.* Minneapolis: Lerner Publications, 2019.

Leaf, Christina. *Doctors.* Minneapolis: Bellwether Media, 2018.

Index

bandages, 19

casts, 19

exam table, 8

medicine, 20

stethoscope, 11

white coat, 7

X-ray, 16

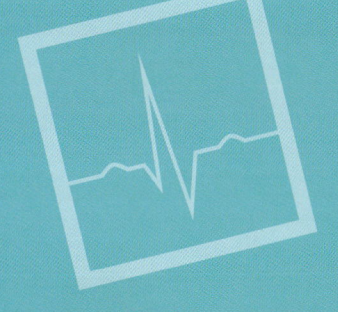

Photo Credits

Image credits: Colin Anderson Productions Pty Ltd/Getty Images, p. 5; Zivica Kerkez/Shutterstock.com, p. 6; Hero Images/Getty Images, pp. 8, 9, 13, 23; Thomas Barwick/Getty Images, p. 10, 23; wavebreakmedia/Shutterstock.com, p. 14; Blend Images - Klaus Tiedge/Getty Images, pp. 16, 17; Steve Debenport/Getty Images, p. 18, 23; Borodach/Getty Images, p. 21; Rob Byron/Shutterstock.com, p. 22; YUCELOZBER/Getty Images, p. 22; sumire8/Shutterstock.com, p. 22; Focus and Blur/Shutterstock.com, p. 22; adamkaz/Getty Images, p. 23.

Cover Images: Sandra van der Steen/Shutterstock.com; ittipon/Shutterstock.com; Creative Crop/Getty Images; Hero Images/Getty Images.